boats against the current

issue I

fall 2022

Copyright © November 26, 2022 by *boats against the current*™

All rights reserved.

No portion of this book may be reproduced in any form without written permission from the publisher or author, except as permitted by U.S. copyright law.

table of contents

editor's note

poet features

starboard under canvas & **telesthesia** / 25-26
Sarah Wallis

the hush & **clam diggers** / 27-28
Pamela Nocerino

sunset in Guanacaste & **winter** & **desire** / 29-31
William G. Gillespie

to the woman who stayed & **the snow that came in October** / 32-33
Lulu Liu

sculpted & **blue** / 34-35
Liz Pino Sparks

[travelers unwashed] & **levity and gravity** / 36-37
Moira Walsh

organic history & **demise** / 38-39
Carella Keil

lost fishermen, from the port of New Bedford & **menopause swings its golden shovel, knocking me into a sweeping drift of lavender** / 40-41
Candice Kelsey

hail to the mothers & **i envy birds** & **his song** / 42-45
Karina Fantillo

ginger tea & **brain hijack** & **of dance and dust** / 46-50
Melanie Taing

wobble & **baggage** / 51-52
Shari Lawrence Pfleeger

fallings & **once** / 53-56
Rebecca Siegel

self-portrait with future scar / 57-58
Lisa Bickmore

dandelions & **red fox** & **early snow** / 59-61
Emily Updegraff

listening for rain & **elegy in silence** / 62-63
Laura Bonazzoli

how to fall & **elevator** & **voyage** / 64-66
Kelli Weldon

translations

[between heaven and earth] & **[poppy petals]** / 71-73
Sonja Crone

another portrait / 75
Ivan de Monbrison

Séidh / 77
Clara McShane

poems

banyan trees / 83
Peter Chiu

nest / 84
Lisa Molina

weeds / 85
M.R. Mandell

this morning / 86
Jose Hernandez Diaz

ode to the fruit of paradise / 87
Natalie Bühler

summer heat / 88
Jeannie Marschall

an ode to the creek in my backyard / 89
Gina Gidaro

stripped back / 90
Debbie Robson

the lengthened, light-filled days / 91
Kathryn Sadakierski

it's getting late / 92-93
Beth Mulcahy

nature walk / 94
Sean Patrick

winter / 95
Kara Dunford

the month after I disappear / 96
C. Heyne

shaw's bridge / 97
Jessica Berry

a new york city coffee shop / 98
Ryan Diaz

metropolis song / 99
Carver Bain

riverside / 100
Louis Faber

indigo blue / 101
Kimberly Reiss

in which an obituary forces me to contemplate life / 102
Erica Abbott

words they use in hospitals / 103-104
Annie Marhefka

the elephant in the room / 105
Emma Lara Jones

vultures / 106
Doryn Herbst

dirt, ash, bone / 107
Devon Bohm

ghosts / 108
Alexis Renata

a horse departs / 109
Bill Richardson

newsworthy / 110
Dave Clark

things left behind / 111
Jordan Bryant

alma / 112
Melody Rose Serra

two candles / 113
Burt Rashbaum

runaway / 114
Eben E. B. Bein

oh body! / 115
Emily Moon

keeper of the shelter tree / 116-117
Chad Norman

domesticus tranquilis / 118-119
John Dorroh

remembering the island / 120
Sarah Burns

[the faerie's ring] / 121-122
Sarah Alarcio

shadorma #1 / 123
P.Christine

looking for clues / 124
Robert Pegel

but I digress / 125
Todd Matson

amygdala / 126
John Tessitore

our place / 127
Sandra Salinas Newton

pineapple stain / 128
Eric Burgoyne

the muse's knot / 129
Karla Linn Merrifield

Zeus' garden / 130
Amir Deen

six trips to Sirius / 131
Adora Williams

centaurs in honey / 132
Daniel A. Rabuzzi

the olive caper / 133
Lisa MacKenzie

favorite beverage / 134
Logan Roberts

aromantic aromatic / 135
R Hamilton

noting nothing / 136
Viktor Tanaskovski

box / 137
Terra Kestrel

I am the spell / 138
Maura Alia Badji

an ode to my first internet friend / 139
Kelli Lage

you wish a heartbeat would suffice / 140
Samikchhya Bhusal

past life lighthouse / 141 - 142
Megan Gahart

my children will be dead before their 50th birthday / 143
Sarah Groustra

mending / 144
Katie E. Peckham

to a whale bobbing rhythmically in the surf / 145
Jacob Riyeff

madam ocean / 146
Krista Bergren-Walsh

harvest moon haibun / 147
Nicole Callräm

stars / 148
Kerry Darbishire

biographies

editor's note

dear reader,

welcome to *boats against the current*! whether you're a poet, writer, contributing author, or poetry lover reading this in a bookstore, we're glad you're here.

at *boats*, our mission is to cultivate an inclusive and safe space where poets from all backgrounds and all stages of their writing journeys can share their work and celebrate beautiful, vulnerable words. the life of a poet can feel isolating at times, but over the course of the past year, we've had the honor of meeting and becoming friends with incredible poets from around the world — many of whom are included in this issue.

if you're new to our poetry magazine, our name comes from this line of *The Great Gatsby* by F. Scott Fitzgerald: "So we beat on, boats against the current, borne back ceaselessly into the past." as the final line of a novel brimming with themes of memory, the past, identity, isolation, and mortality, we feel as though it's the perfect name for a poetry magazine that seeks to explore these topics — among others — in new ways. we live to publish poems that take everyday feelings and experiences and turn them into words, images, and lines that delight.

we started *boats against the current* on October 26th, 2021, looking forward to publishing poems, establishing a name for ourselves, and becoming part of the poetry community. now, exactly one year and one month later, we're excited to present you with our very first *boats against the current* poetry collection. these poets will take you on a journey through nature, reincarnation, introspection, loss, grief, healing, relationships, vulnerability, and the sea (our favorite), among many other topics. enjoy reading!

warmly,

McKenna Themm

editor-in-chief, *boats against the current*
november 26th, 2022

poet features

starboard under canvas
Sarah Wallis

Imagine a tent,
old style, heavy canvas and ropes
that sing shanties in the wind —

it's like being on a sailing ship,
cast adrift at night in a mad bundle
of old rigging, the sails all mildew
and must, the boards not oiled,
the mizzen left to rot, mainsail
not patched but the movement
holds steady in the well known swell,

host the colours — port out, starboard
home — and tread light, sleep well

for I sail this ship in my dreams.

telesthesia
Sarah Wallis

we have no language for this silent
sea that laps, to slip the shore, to and fro,
hides an understanding that slides between us,

only wanting to stay the moment when we
might sink into willing arms, pliant
as a weeping willow, only, do not fill

this vessel with tears and drown us both,

take courage, and row the boat again, with
your two lips seeking out the oars of mine

the hush
Pamela Nocerino

hush
hush
of rhythmic waves
uncover and bury
the shells of the lives I imagined
& the life I carry —
the space between as vast and blurry
as the crepuscular horizon.
Wet lines of tide mark
what was and what will be again.
My faltering steps,
a moment at best,
fill with sea and retreat
as I embrace the light dullness
of essential insignificance.

clam diggers
Pamela Nocerino

Hidden muscles fold and bend
like accordions
to dig in mourning sand.
Dawn reveals stretched, wide belly creases
in briefly upright shore hunters
who decide what to keep and
what to release —
a bewitching sort
to witness —
alike, in its way,
to memories
locked tight and left buried
without heat
to open and consume,
like mussels,
for tomorrow's bending.

sunset in Guanacaste
William G. Gillespie

In the quietness of the peninsula

I listen to the waves turn white
against the cliffs
against the sun brushing the porcelain sands with gold

there is no sail in sight
save the frigatebird

rising like an angel
above the bay

taken on a current
I will one day know
toward the mountain veils of green

winter
William G. Gillespie

I see the last of the plum leaves fall
as a gust of wind whistles the end of autumn

soon the shivering window hums
with blue adumbrations of snow and solitude

I chew my mandarin
and listen —

when I gather in my arms
the cold winter winds

I rock to sleep
the promise of spring

desire
William G. Gillespie

The fisherman
plucked a grape

from the crown
of a white wave

but the grape
round and sweet

shriveled
in the salt of his hand

to the woman who stayed
Lulu Liu

The dogwood's been chewed on
again   it won't bloom this year either
yet at the first
breath of spring   you'll bear
the old shovel to its branches
break   the frost-sealed ground
and work a mound of compost
into the   exhale
There's much to do
to tender the   roots
of a human life
and you   have steeped
your tea of   discontent
long enough   too long really
day after lonely   day   over
and over   ducked
the swinging anvil of your
anger   and you're glad to be
past all that   finally
This is the calm that
decision brings
the pain that is the   deep
ripening   has dulled
(an old well   grown over in
the meadow)   leaving
just   a sutured   hollow
Besides   there is always the
pleasure   of the night sky
always   sleep
in his gentle arms   always
the next life

the snow that came in October
Lulu Liu

was not impossible but not expected.

The city had not salted the roads.
There could have easily been

another crop of tomatoes.
We woke to a strange sight:

ice-slumping leaf-heavy branches
all the way to the ground,

the begonias dead
in a shocked, bloody heap –

the perimeters of our lives
having closed a notch tighter –

and stored those among
other images of this year,

all out of order.

         — October 2020

sculpted
Liz Pino Sparks

Jagged, many layers deep, what lives
in the Vyatke? They say fish enter a
kind of stasis, wait out the winter. We

wait out the winter, too, in studios
where we are first looked at
as women. They must be cold, too,

but memory is less clear here. The
old men wait until the ice breaks.
They swim now for everlasting

life. An exchange between them
and an absent god, seventy years
until he returns, and by then they have

forgotten the rituals. Aged hands
sculpt me. For the first time, I
am beautiful. I am not

invited to the funeral. Lofted spaces,
ceilings many stories high. A wife who
brings tea. A soon dead husband

begging marble to take shape into my
first seduction.

Perhaps I killed him.

His head, marble bust, hangs along
the walls, next to mine and forty years
of sacrifices.

blue
Liz Pino Sparks

Most of us hush down, never say a word.
Because   when we say the sky
is blue you tell us   it is not blue and tell us
not to get hysterical. And you tell us
what blue is and, somehow, it is different than
what we thought blue was.   We never knew blue.
What is blue?   So we rip off the
roof so that we will know blue even better, we
paint with only blue,   stroke the cheek of blue
with tender fingers and then,   after a longest day
under roofless blue sky, we finally say again that
the sky is blue.   And you say   we
don't understand blue   and   we will never
understand blue.   Not to worry our little heads
about blue.   Blue is hard   and so much
bigger than us. We should think about something else
and remind us not to get   hysterical.

[travelers unwashed]
Moira Walsh

travelers unwashed
pinched by hunger and cold
the late fall flowers

levity and gravity
Moira Walsh

On this bird-pummeled morn
I heard, You have no voice?
Here, take ours.
So generous.

And the steadfast earth said
Here, my dear,
I have enough heaviness
for both of us.

organic history
Carella Keil

We are but scales to be shed on an infinitely evolving beast, at one moment vital and effervescent, and the next sloughed off. A conscious moment in the organic history of the universe.

demise
Carella Keil

green swandive to the ground/your one perfect pirouette/the shuddering urge to let go/instinct promises/it will be different this time/release isn't a beautiful demise, but only the beginning/let the cold touch/push you over the edge/to the tips of you, where red colors pulse.

lost fishermen, from the port of New Bedford
Candice Kelsey

Melville wrote of bitter blanks on chapel walls, & Crane sang
shadows swallowed by thundering waves. Lowell reported bones

of Quaker boys, Nantucket-drowned in stranded hulks — No one
sings of the *Paolina* downed by a nor'easter; no poets wrote

of '52 when New Bedford lost Fritz Hokanson & crew: Overdue
at shore & lore, the ship sank. Abandoned in Buzzard's Bay:

Twin tankers clove in two like that ship in Hardy's *Twain*;
yet here no whale or iceberg were to blame. The rescue

pulled the Coast Guard cutter *Unimak* to the stern-turned-bow.
Waves of radio & sea bid farewell to *Paolina*'s wood & bones —

Thirty-eight years later, the tragedy off Kelley's Landing.
While fishing for flounder the *Sol e Mar* sinks. Father & son:

William Hokanson Sr. and Jr. plunged after father & grandfather.
Fritz of the *Paolina*-wreck was father to the *Sol's* chief. No woman

endures the curse of generations lost at sea. Shelley's Queen Mab
commands *Sleep!* yet families wake to grief. They sit under salt lips

of cenotaphs for *Sol e Mar*'s dear bones — Who works the iambs
& the lines to honor those dear men? No poets fill these vessels

lost to seas & Coast Guard pleas with a heroic couplet sandbar:
Only silence warbles to the stars of the *Paolina* & *Sol e Mar*.

menopause swings its golden shovel, knocking me into a sweeping drift of lavender
after Kwame Dawes' "Purple"

Candice Kelsey

Sleep is the baby that will not come. I labor the pillow that is too warm, so lumpy
I pray for some doula to relieve me of this nine-month insomnia. I toss it away
for one cool as metal stirrups which held these feet wide to see my daughter's nose
emerge like a spring bulb from weeds and clay. A body asserting purpose aggressively.

The warmth of her tiny palms, baby girl gripping my finger like a flower to smell,
or a future. Both of us intoxicated by new life, unable to sense the thousand what ifs —
nineteen years and I sweat a midnight; three hundred miles away, she cries from wasps
of anxiety, expectation, confusion, and fear this global humbling releases into our air.

I send her an Easter basket, tiny wicker garden of chocolate and raffia, grassy green,
to remind her she is loved. She sends her paper on Henry James' use of the Edenic: you
always know how to fix my writing. She accidentally reminds me I am needed. A wasp
sounds like a purring cat if you listen carefully. Sleep arrives in the cool Georgia rain.

hail to the mothers
Karina Fantillo

trailing scent of gardenias
soft-packed earth & mint
refreshing how she curls
her belly to shelter a seed
growing inside a live new
heart beating her rhythm

like a mama great gray
devoutly sitting on her eggs
for a month until they hatch
under her bare brood patch
tidying the nest   eating
her chicks' cracked shells

yields her body as a vessel
bearing the ancestral line
knowing only she can carry
succession from extinction
she mirrors the divine
in her reflection

mothers split   open
to let in the light   & summon
a breeze   so we   can rise

his song

Karina Fantillo

lone sparrow croons
me awake shuddering
my window wailing
his song at 5 am
urgent as breath

he cascades
downpour of trills
piercing louder
i wonder
does anyone hear —

yowls ricochet
in a chasm
inside my fault
lines i cling
over the edge

as the notes knit
morning mist
electricity singes
ruptured heart
flickering it on

i envy birds

Karina Fantillo

migrating to summer &
winter spots perennially
traversing with flocks
who may not be family
internal clock ticking
aligned with the sun
unlike my biological clock
that never got wound
no 5- or 10-year plan
no passports required
no one saying *you don't belong*

when leaves turn
cryptochromes guide
toward lit blue
magnetic fields
pulsing through
earth to center
for the crossing
where some will expire
retiring to the universe

how i long
to unfurl wings
buoying my body
a skidding coot
skimming the water
like skipping stones
then i'd beat & quiver
the air & let the sky
swallow my glide
coasting an updraft
inside me a compass

as i soar at home
       wherever i go

ginger tea
Melanie Taing

I was always too afraid
to tell you that I hated
the taste
of the ginger tea
that you claim keeps
you kicking all these years.

Not the kicking
off concrete, coasting,
the forward motion of your wheels over
ramps and stairs and metal bars,
not even the speed
traps could deter
you. I sensed, still, hanging
from your shoulders, my cheek
against your stubble, the silent
crests of a sine
wave you omitted.

Not the six mile
runs along the coast, cross
fit sessions until you vomit,
famished, penance
perhaps, the ghosts
of which you hid under
layers of ink
beneath your skin.

I read courage
a million times
over because I felt everything
but. Your indecision
skinning me

into a submission too much
like my living room.

Still, I swallowed, sipped,
savored,
the aftertaste
an interruption —
        — a foreign flavor, a taste
I wondered whether
you ever really
acquired.

brain hijack
Melanie Taing

My chest is a 40-ton semi-truck, collapsed.
Catastrophe in a Chinese finger trap.
It's all the same pink fleshy slimy bits of brain.
It must be the coffee.

Catastrophe in a Chinese finger trap.
I want to be strong, but I am strung out; unravelling.
It must be the coffee.
Well-oiled machines know no rest, do they?

I want to be strong, but I am strung out; unravelling.
I can't sleep, Tetris in my sheets.
Well-oiled machines know no rest, do they?
Do I take up too much space?

I can't sleep, Tetris in my sheets.
It's all the same pink fleshy slimy bits of brain.
Do I take up too much space?
My chest is a 40-ton semi-truck, collapsed.

of dance and dust
Melanie Taing

Little apsara,
whose fingers are guided
by the Gods
with the vitality of
one thousand
lightning bolts,
whose spine sways
with the spirit
of the naga
ready to strike,
whose hips hold
the fertility of the land
and the progeny
of our people,
whose curves carve
rivers into the earth and
summon rains
for the crop,
whose smile
signifies
the bridge between
heaven and earth,
the tongue of
nature,
tendril,
tree,
leaf,
flower,
fruit,
rebirth.

Little apsara,
a relic,

a plea to the heavens,
hands always pointed
in prayer,
whose poise portrays
the divine detachment
of the deities,
who were soundless
when they slaughtered
our people.

Little apsara,
whose bones bear
the burden
of our history,
whose weary muscles
and frame buckles
under the pressure of
her inheritance,
whose sealed smile
signifies
the bridge between
heaven and earth,
the grace of a rage
for the root
that was too soon
returned to dust.

wobble
Shari Lawrence Pfleeger

As Earth's axis leans lazily back from the Sun,
in easy duality North and South Poles
diametrically tug at Earth's in-between.
Molten iron rises toward crusty outer skin,
then oozes back toward center, making Poles shimmy
and shift, their movement teasing magnets and maps.
As glaciers and polar ice soften, melt,
move as liquid through surging seas,
our spinning orb wobbles, jounces
and judders, unsteadily trundles
through space and time. Like a tottering toddler,
puffy, pliant legs quaking, vibrating,
straining to move through the world. Like the jittering
of hand-cranked film, or the doddering, jiggling snow
just before the avalanche plummets, carpeting the valley
in suffocatingly shimmering glitter. Like my mother,
when her comfortable, overstuffed-chair world
quivered, when her brain wobbled and wept,
when the life she sought
became the life she dreaded,
when her daughters, polar opposites,
became her North Star.

baggage
Shari Lawrence Pfleeger

Transition complete, chairs folded and stacked,
funeral done, remains encoffined and
tucked in their hypogeal home, sorrow
swelling, I unwind his involute life.
Father gone, I empty shoe boxes, drawers
and kitchen cabinets, tag tokens, sift
painful from poignant, place revealed secrets
in protective wrapping, in easy reach.
But what of loose detritus: words that stung
but comfort now, disturbing artifacts
that later might uplift? How much to keep,
to hold aloft, wear proudly, carry on?
I need no footlocker: just his watch and
compass. I fill a holdall with his laugh.

fallings
Rebecca Siegel

Night fell and the moon
pulled us tight to her

chest then rain then snow
took what was left

of the leaves with fall
leaving the rutted path

rusted the chickadees
took their plunge

from the birch to
the feeder little

death defiers tiny
fliers in December's

smudge of fog it's
unseemly unseasonably

warm say the scientists
says the bear drawn

out of slumber by this
strange summer called

by what remains under
the apple tree the black

oil sunflower droppings
sumac berries our

defenseless trash can
now disemboweled

its organs scattered
down the driveway

we pick up what we
threw away rock

forward with each
step we could fall

into something new
the solstice is nearly

here neatly splitting
the year we could

run, we could go
fast enough to

become airborne
but for this gravity

ashes and smoke
things fall awake

in love
asleep
apart

once
Rebecca Siegel

I was a patient with a lump
in my throat the doctor touched
me so tenderly but I knew his
love was for the nodule his fine
needle aspired to pierce his
desire to know the strange cells
of my uncharted sea I had never
been so adored as I was those
weeks when I was open to
the gaze of those quick machines
my throat thrown back in abandon
I fell in love with my surgeon's
hands that knew how deep to cut
to keep a girl from floating
from her life

why this has come back to
me today I don't know except
how aware I am that nothing
stays and yet nothing goes
things we once worried over
so much slipped behind us
and were lost in the wake of
days only to wash up one
rain-speckled morning in
October between the last
of the orange leaves on the
little cherry tree, the path
tiled with bad news — Once

we saw a ship in full sail slide
along the silent beach as the
sun slapped the waves and

we watched from the dune
the dog spinning in ecstasy
and our arms not strong
enough to hold the day's
kite we let it slip from our
hands the truth is we didn't
notice it was gone until it was
too late the scar on my throat
is pale now only visible if
you're close enough to hold me
or harm me.

self-portrait with future scar
Lisa Bickmore

first I remove the cloud at my throat, loop
de looped out of silver wire in a shape
like dread, like drift and weather: then see doctors,

three of them, who've found the thing there,
the little knot: to be palpated by
expert hands, or aspirated by fine needle,

or taken by knife: *that's a nodule,* says the first.
the second, aspirator, asks *how are you doing, ma'am?*
my neck exposed under a bright lamp:

and because of cells, a few too many
of the wrong kind — spring fluke, heat flare
— the surgeon tells me, *there's a chance,*

very small, that we might nick the
recurrent laryngeal nerve, and thus
I might lose my voice, for a little while

or forever: *I need my voice,* I tell him, before
they drug me, *don't wreck it*: before
the sleep, its wooly veil: I wake

and before I know myself, I
struggle with the nurse, so she will not
remove my restraints: then relents, gives

me water to sip from a cup,
sluicing down. *I need my voice,*
I tell myself in a whisper,

for singing, for sharp speaking, for
naming the tempest swelling in
the sky, and everywhere: at the hollow,

a strip of white tape delimits
the length of the cut, stitches holding
edges together where it will knit,

dissolve into a thin pale seam: healing,
I sit at the window, the red
maple unfurling its florid leaves.

dandelions
Emily Updegraff

She proudly offers me
  a handful of dandelions

Of course I do not
  tell her they're weeds

that not all flowers are beautiful
  Adults actually think such things

She finds them delightful
  in school-bus yellow

Downy pom-poms
  set to flight by pursed lips

They return regardless
  of last year's efforts at elimination

Taproot, parachute seed
  promiscuous pollination

the elements of their persistence
  So if she loves them let it be

not just for beauty, but for strategy
  Drink deep, sail high

choose your seat
  and sit down

red fox
Emily Updegraff

As the last ribbons of blush fade from the sky, I see
her sprawled on a neighbor's lawn. Slender snout,
alert ears, dark legs, lively tail. She watches me
from a few paces away. Perhaps I should fear her
but I do not. She lifts a paw, scratches her head
just the way my dog does. I have seen her before,
at the end of her hunting hours, before traffic starts up,
before children fill the sidewalks.

Something wild, even in this neighborhood.

Foxes are spirit guides, my sister informs me, they
indicate change. The end of a difficult time. I want
the plague to end, a sunburn to peel off my skin,
to quit my job and start over, I want a hard thunderstorm,
a bonfire, new love, something wild but familiar to show up
and remind me who I am. The fox means change
she says, but signs have failed me before and
I'll be damned before I'm tricked again.

early snow
Emily Updegraff

Down the road from home, flowers
gold in summer, now the color of toast,
stand over early November snow.

On her own, walking the road before
it snowed, she overlooked them, at home
against toasted grass and leaves of gold.

She nearly takes them, these flowers dry
as toast, down the snowy road and back home.
So-called golden years. Saved for, spent alone.

listening for rain
Laura Bonazzoli

All summer, the trees waited:
leafstalks drooping,
blades wilting,
stomates — little mouths — closed
even at night.

Early,
their chlorophyll retreating,
the leaves changed to red and gold.
Some shed green acorns —
stunted fruits.

Now in the rising wind
their dry branches scrape
like fiddlers' bows
scratching a *Dies Irae*
upon the heavy sky.

All summer, I wanted to believe
the prognosticators' maps and graphs,
their sketches of deciduous trees:
leaves, trunk, feeder roots,
rain.

Now who can say whether or not
the rusty blackbird might ever return,
whether children born perhaps last summer
might someday trace a pathway home
through these woods?

elegy in silence
Laura Bonazzoli

After the power goes out
and the room is stunned mute,

I grope for a candle, strike and blow out
a match, and conjure words to recreate you

for your elegy, but the silence
keens its own words, so

I set the candle aside, watch the shadows
animate the walls, and think

of Plato's cave and wonder if somehow
you could be alive somewhere

out there beyond the flames, or if
ten billion galaxies are as far as it all goes

and if they'd be enough to see by
if the candle were to flicker out. Then

I snuff the candle out,
rise, and walk in the now vaster darkness,

feeling my way along the cooling walls toward
wherever the silence beckons me to go.

how to fall
Kelli Weldon

slope alongside Sam Houston state park trails
dry Louisiana oak leaves crunch under age 8 weight
quiet cacophony as her little body rolls
quickly
down
then steadies
sun through the trees
a lightweight Sisyphus emerging.

that's the right way to fall,
arms crossed over your heart to guard it.
just like it is, even now
when the ground gives out underneath
and you oblige
you have to hold on to yourself.

elevator
Kelli Weldon

our time arrives
days stretch out within this minute
a raindrop suspended, teeming with microbes.
gravity tugs your heels to Earth,
you straighten your spine
cables and counterweights abide
a nod of recognition.

my stomach sinks, the eerie knot subsides.
maybe you knew me in another life.

down and down
and straight ahead
be careful
this is all we get.

voyage
Kelli Weldon

boat engine turning over
gulls in the wind
a song I have never heard.
Adventure beckons
the cold, dark thrill
the deep
wonders
seize the current, surprise my anchor.
"yes," I am whispering before I can stop myself
"yes" to the storm that is brewing.

translations

[between heaven and earth]
Sonja Crone

between heaven and earth
between the lines
my deep sea
washes around torn words
carries fragments with pleasure
until sense again
until breath

Zwischen Himmel und Erde
zwischen den Zeilen
mein tiefes Meer
umspült zerrissene Worte
trägt Silben mit Lust
bis wieder Sinn
bis Atem

[poppy petals]
Sonja Crone

poppy petals
red sun chords
tied in hair

Mohnblumenblätter
rote Sonnenakkorde
gebunden im Haar

another portrait
Ivan de Monbrison

A child's murder
or something
like this
a living nightmare
you put
the night in a bottle
to use it as ink
to draw your own portrait
on a piece of paper

другой портрет

Убийство ребенка
Или что-то
Как это
Кошмар наяву
Ты положил
Ночь в бутылке
Она служит твоими чернилами
Нарисовать свой автопортрет
На листе бумаги

séidh
Clara McShane

I often believe that the Irish for blow – Séidh
speaks softly to the fragrant song of the breeze.
Séidh hushes fondly each cluster of trees.
Blow is a ruler, a faux-God, a brute.
Voluminous, mighty and red–
Wind does not blow each clover bed.
Wind is a spirited force,
and blow is human, hollow to the wistful ear.
Wind cannot blow what it does not fear.
When mighty gusts sweep over craggy fields of gorse,
secrets of the sídhe are scattered over sheets of yellow glow.
Whispers of faeries too wilful to blow.
Off the coast of Malin Head, somewhere in the starry sea,
a piece of driftwood is shunted along by the gentle breath of the fish.
Bí ag séideadh, cairde airgid, bí ag séideadh anois.

Sídhe — a supernatural race in Celtic mythology (an older form of sí).
Bí ag séideadh, cairde airgid, bí ag séideadh anois — "Blow, silver friends, blow now."

poems

banyan trees
Peter Chiu

In another life, we were probably banyan trees
        growing tall enough to see the land around us,
sleeping through nights heavy as smoke.

        We can see past the ridgeline separating us
from the other side where a field of marigolds bloom.
        A lark down below gathers herself for flight

over the wide mouth of a river. She is the translator
        collecting all our words, forming them
into something worthy for flight. But who knew

        about the grief in her wings — her body laden
with morning dew as she glided past the ridgeline.
        She soon disappears as we watch on anxiously,

waiting for a cobweb of amber light,
        and maybe that's when we'll speak
to the grief left in our bodies.

nest
Lisa Molina

hatched thatched threads
shoot as arrows;
the neural dendrites

connecting, surrounding
my gray matter, while
skeleton twigs float

down down down
onto the branch, wet
from crimson rain,

or is it blood
that keeps my
nest intact?

weeds
M.R. Mandell

so many stories about roses
and daffodils, we forget

to honor the weeds. misfits
we pull, never pick.

awkward flowers we place in
trash cans, never a child's hands.

their deeds unnoticed,
they never complain.

how they nourish the soil,
so beauty can flourish.

how they pluck water from
the sky, so gardens can grow.

how they sacrifice their lives
for the pretty, and the green.

this morning
Jose Hernandez Diaz

after W.S. Merwin

The sun comes through the window like a bird to a tree
        I rise bloom again something free for once it can't
Change this time I'll hold tight the steering wheel

        In this moment between a star and a galaxy we
Part when I go downstairs to make scrambled eggs
        With tortillas and ketchup like a blue-collar Mexican-

American coffee no milk just sugar I remember
        The words my mother said when she was going
To start a new job she said a challenge is not something

        To fear walk through the door with your head
Held high learn but lead soon it will be routine
        This life like truth like love is a puzzle

ode to the fruit of paradise
Natalie Bühler

For a few Tuesdays, it's just the three
of us: my mother, the grapefruit and me.
She holds it, the size of my head,
steady to cut it in half, unleashing the entire

ten minutes of quiet it holds underneath
its moon surface. Using the serrated knife
with the curved blade, she then loosens
each segment just enough for my spoon,

sprinkles dark sugar to cut through
what she thinks is a sickly aftertaste.
My mind is all pink flesh, segments
within segments holding treasure,

popping teardrop cells with my tongue
against the roof of my mouth, sweetness
sticking hair to my cheeks. She pretends
not to watch, tuts as my sleeves dip

into the juice on my plate. Later,
I pray, next to the half-built crib in my
dark room: to the patron saint
of messy children — please, remake

the fruit of paradise
into a neat little mandarin.

summer heat
Jeannie Marschall

I sit sunshine
on sparse grass,
sensing, existing;
I swear the earth has a heartbeat,
slow as time, bright as lizard scales,
grace as a red kite passing long
breath flowing slowly into cracks, through
trunks, ghosting over diaphanous wings flitting
goosebumps as my toes tickle the dust.
Someone always muses, *why*
don't you put on some shoes as
aren't you scared
you might step into something;
I have to confess I am confused, why
don't you take them off?
You might step into feeling.

an ode to the creek in my backyard
Gina Gidaro

Here is to that lapping of green and brown,
that splash of uncertainty,
wave of familiarity. You are the
host of summer's biggest party,
inviting bathing suits, picnic baskets,
and sunscreen to your nature-made mansion.
With boiling hot sand between the toes of your guests
and the cloudless blue skies over their heads,
the local pool could never offer turtle sightings
and seashell pickings. Your waters are free-flowing, soft,
ever changing, you remain at ease. The creek bed will
praise your name regardless of the
banks you chip away. The trees and the scrubs
know their place among your dusky
shadows, reaching their roots
for you to clench onto, for you to
mold around. Your currents
hold the stories of years gone by,
of generations seen, time spent,
shoes lost, bonds unbent —
and who wouldn't want to be a part of that
even if it was meant to slip right
through our insatiable hands?

stripped back
Debbie Robson

The land is fenced off these days. Where homes
stood is now a green/brown field guarded by a
solitary she-oak. Peaceful on this sunny afternoon.

Impossible to imagine the dead-end road with
traffic lights blinking. With motorists waiting for
green to ascend the main street and go on their way.

How many houses have gone? Two, four or
six? Are the foundations still there below
the grass, reverberating? Seeking out

the lost dimensions of walls and roof.
To recreate voices, music, tv shows. School
children shouting above the idling cars.

Beyond, traffic streams past the truncated incline.
Was it ever that steep? I try to imagine myself
back there, waiting for the lights to change.

I try to recall the lost houses either side of me.
But I am at the fence and can't go back. Some things
are incomprehensible. Only the landscape knows.

the lengthened, light-filled days
Kathryn Sadakierski

the clouds are cherry blossoms
floating in the sky
with fading wisps of spring daylight.

their reflections flicker like swimming fish
in the water of the reservoir
as though ruffled by wind.

a mirror image, an illusion
is just as fragile
as the down of dandelion.

it changes just as quickly
as the colors of the trees,
which are like snakes that shed their skin,
butterflies in a constant state of metamorphosis,
red-gold wings like apple slices
descending to the earth.

it's getting late
Beth Mulcahy

It's getting late
in August. again
you can tell from
fly-covered mice belly up
on the sidewalk and shriveled
hanging basket flower pots on porches
you can feel it slap your face if
you don't duck from
storm soaked leaves of limbs needing trimmed
that hang over the path
you can see it in the height of the corn of course
and smell it in sharpened pencils and plastic new containers

It's getting late
in the day
on Sunday. again
and things can't be held off anymore
so the inevitability of time running out
is thick in its film of imminence
but you keep thinking about the white clouds in a dark blue sky at midnight
on summer solstice in Scotland

It's getting late
in life. by now
you can tell by the way your knee yells
and the white wiry hair popping up on your head
and the way it feels like there isn't enough time
to notice things like you should
like really good aged cheddar and

it's getting late
in the summer. now
and the way the air feels

when you move through it is like it moves through you
washing into your face with a freshness that
makes you take off your glasses so you can fully feel
every bit of it on every bit of you
while you try to take a picture
of the way it feels when the air starts to get cool like this
when it's getting late. again

nature walk
Sean Patrick

I've walked these rocky trails
before. I've spent time among the
trees. They have wonders
and hidden things:
a frog who croaks away the
fall, a cedar
creaking in the wind, a shadow
casting a lonely pall
over a back road's dusty
end. Ephemera lie in this wood,
these things that are
won't be again — these phantoms green,
these spirits of the spring's devising.
And soon, a winter moon will rise.

winter
Kara Dunford

When the snow cascades
down, unrelenting and
cold, I study

the evergreen, branches
weighed down by the
weather, yet standing

tall, anchored in
her roots, soaring
toward the sky.

Year upon year she
greets me, steady in
her syllables, constant in

her hue. Telling her holy
story, and ever thus.

the month after I disappear
C. Heyne

the pavement outside
my apartment

is repatched
& the hallway still

smells of mold. I'm
nostalgic for fungi

& wonder what I
must look like now

mirrors all patched up,
when did reflection

start to scare me? Sometimes
I'll catch myself in a puddle

or in the distort of bathwater
& wonder where time's gone

shaw's bridge
Jessica Berry

Come off the A24, onto Mealough Road
You'll land in Shaw's Bridge. The place my father died.
I didn't travel there myself until twenty years after,
Afraid of too much caustic knowledge eroding my last memories of him
Smiling outside The Coachman; lowering into a skinny, red car,
Telling mum and I never to worry about Monday's appointment.
"Hospital?" "Sorry, no. Not hospital. I meant to say doctor."
We never got to ask him if he lied to throw our anxiety some spare change.
Absorbing the pummelled path, the froggy water, the trees
So lime the air tasted like sour candy, was a telescope
Back in time. In this small world, significance beats in the wings
Of all things. I sucked the juice out of every dizzy step without
Breaking the fragile peel. It felt scary. Listening to his bass voice,
Birch leaves bouncing back the last conversation,
Watching kids listing dangerously close to river edges,
Wondering if he knew the same fears.
I saw him walking the opposite direction, towards us.
My father, suddenly come alive again. Not fanciful, but flesh and blood under shade.
I stole across the mud trail at him. Then tripped on a tree's big foot; looked up to the
Empty space I've always known. These days, we keep having these clandestine
Alliances. Midnight drives, we spy each other through headlight mist.
An unbidden guest in the attic, searching through rubbish tips
To find the last of his smell: musk and apple.
I press demo on my electric piano; Arabesque No. 1 plays,
This is the soundtrack of my childhood: the sound of Stephen's heart swelling,
Touching the brims and exploding. Ready to claim a spot in the sky's ballroom,
To take his own parents in arms for a dance.
His head landed where my soles skimmed. Barely open eyes watched
Birds dotting clouds:
The black and white keys. A revolving door. An unfinished melody.

a new york city coffee shop
Ryan Diaz

Walled in on either side by layers of red brick
People quietly sip their coffee
And ignore the mailman dragging his bag behind his back,

Neither looking at the other,
Staring into their coffee cups
Like Narcisuss bending over his pool,

Everyone lost in their own little worlds —
Geocentrists foolishly believing
Themselves to be the sun.

metropolis song
Carver Bain

   I grow
both older and wider.
I fill the valley and climb the hill,
building factories and mills
and I consume the earth —
the pines, the sky, and stones;
I turn them toward my girth
as though I am stronger. Yet
I know nothing of strength
nor depth. Though I might say
a word on length, the grass
could tell you more.

      How I would soar
         if I could. But, I am older than you
and heavier too. I am made
for nothing but dying, old
as soon as I'm new. To the birds
and the leaves, the men and the trees,
oh how I would become you. How
I would color and bend
in spring. How I would shiver
in fall,

          but as I have said
with the cracks in the sidewalk,
the sign on the store, the moss
up on rooftops, the creak of a door,
I was made for dying,
                nothing more.

riverside
Louis Faber

They sit this morning much as they
have sat each day for more
than half a century, waiting
on the Danube river wall.

Many stare across the water
see Old Buda and the Bastion,
others peer anxiously up
at St Stephens Basilica,
all remembering and waiting.

In the evening they hear
the approach of feet, wonder
if theirs will arrive finally,
know that they are gone, are now
yet another footnote in a dark
atrocity that no one can forget,
and the short, final walk
from the Dohany Street Synagogue,
prayer books left on seats,
and they hear the river
that carried their souls away.

indigo blue
Kimberly Reiss

If my world crumbles,
and I lose everything,
wrap me in a well-worn and weighty blanket,
feed me briny oysters, big chunks of watermelon,
and hot chai tea.
Let's agree to let the pregnant past hang,
like the plumpest of purple grapes
almost ready for picking.
Watch me sleep, let time inch by,
tip-toe up close
and make sure I'm still breathing.
It won't matter that yours is an island of one,
that there's never enough room for another,
at least not for very long.
Like a transistor radio coming in and out of range,
the other heard only in short, staticky, spurts.
How l longed for that station to just stay put,
so we could dance to the whole song.
But that could never be,
not on an island of one,
surrounded by all that deep indigo blue.

in which an obituary forces me to contemplate life
Erica Abbott

Two knives and a fork sit in the sink. Spoons are nowhere to be found. This is not a gentle haunting. Your ghost is still everywhere [and] nowhere when I try to see you. You're a thief, stealing your scent from the air the minute I try to reach, to see if touch is still a sense that belongs to us. At night, you burn out every last streetlight until all but what can be seen keeps me moving. Sparks fly overhead and I'm tempted to stand beneath the tiny fires just to feel the sting. I'd grab bees straight off flowers if I had to. When I say I don't know how to go on, I mean I only ever see half a map. You Are *(not)* Here. Take me somewhere I can see the stars. An anechoic chamber for sight, if you will. There is so much light here. I keep poems in the trunk of my car in case of emergency. Lord, let me feel beyond the beyond. You're becoming holy again. A saintly seduction preys itself around my neck and the sins come pouring out. Wherever you are, I hope you've found [ ]. My veins refuse to feed organs some days, scavenge my own blood like a predator unto myself. I was always taught a *then* must always follow an *if* so if this is all a simulation then let it be a deadening. I have never seen an ocean I didn't want to walk across, never touched tombstones without wanting to put a telephone booth next door. Who's it for? I can't be sure these days. I'd bury myself if not for me. I want this grief to gnaw me down to the marrow's atom. Isn't it true we are all one inhale away from never knowing another mirrored exhale. [?]

words they use in hospitals
Annie Marhefka

comfort measures
I don't hate the term as much
as I should, or as much
as I loathe other phrases
that embed in foreheads
like initials in concrete.

It is softer than
do not resuscitate
silkier, kinder, more
humane, like a bed of
autumn leaves and not
an intubation hose.

It is more fleeting than
advanced directives
unfinished, in motion, less
final, like a hummingbird
that darts and hovers and not
a document signed at deathbedside.

It is more infinite than
end-of-life
stretching, lasting, not
bookended like a bamboo stalk
that climbs into ceiling-less sky and not
the cessation of breath.

comfort measures
like the steam from chicken noodle soup,
a brush of soft fingertip
to shoulder blade,
a squeeze of a palm,

release.

the elephant in the room
Emma Lara Jones

My brother was the source
of all wild mischief.
Stampeding through the house
he'd overturn large furniture,
daub mud on bathroom walls,
rip wallpaper off with his tusks.
Hiding upstairs we'd listen
to his rumbled calls: thrilled
and scared at his wild revolt.

Eventually he had to leave:
the walls too thin and weak
to withstand the rumpus.
Now and again he'd
return; his feet making craters
in our living room floor.
We'd cover the holes with a rug
and learn to skirt around
them – the air rich
with his fragrant musth.

vultures
Doryn Herbst

The first birds to circle
beckon their friends.

Vultures have the beak
to peel back the skin
of an elephant, the stomach
to swallow and break down
infested flesh.

Without these acts, thousands
upon thousands of beasts
would rot in open graves,
leaching malady into the earth.

Vultures of the human kind
do not wait for their victims
to be dead.

dirt, ash, bone
Devon Bohm

I like to think about St. Francis preaching to the birds,
calling them his sisters, their graceful wings alighting
on the friar, claws clean through the rough spun cassock.
My aunt has a statue of this moment in her garden.
Half my father's ashes are scattered around that small,
stone figure — you can see it from her kitchen window.
The fishbones in the fertilizer have changed the hydrangeas
over from pink into blue this year — pale, like a rime
of ice or skin of milk of the sky in a season where flowers
never bloom. I don't make a habit of prayer, but, if I did,
this is what I would pray to: the way raspberries cup
their bodies on the vine, filling up with juice, the crack
of fennel seeds between my teeth, the bronze sunlight
in the late afternoon falling across the face of a reasonable
man standing watch over someone I know loved me.
The deft hum of dragonfly, the bored survival of crows,
the natural selection that led to this moment where all
are gravely divine, all are what St. Francis meant when
he told the world: *It is in pardoning that we are pardoned.
You have no enemy except yourselves.* Gored by
growing older, impaled by forgetting, remembering
forgiveness, above all else, is the only way to honor you.
The statue's face is weathered, but I can still see his eyes,
can still see the flowers pushing their way up through
the thin, shivering stratum of dirt, ash, bone.

ghosts
Alexis Renata

maybe you're right &
ghosts don't exist
but consider the boy
dead ten years still

visiting my dreams,
still telling me about his
day, a day that doesn't exist.
consider the apple

left on the office desk
the night before the plague,
uneaten. consider the box
in the garage collecting

dust, & all that it holds,
& all that it doesn't. consider
the way the smell of rain
lingers after the clouds

have gone, the way the river
swells after the snow has
melted. consider, if you will,
the dead oak tree still standing,

not yet cut down, looking almost
alive in the morning sun.

a horse departs
Bill Richardson

It's been ages since you left
and still I get these crazy dreams.
A huge white mechanical horse
— even the saddle and the bridle were white,
the stirrups and the reins –
and you, the rider, grinning and saying
something — wait, what was it? Oh yes,
about the way it's normal now
to travel around town
on such a steed, you said.
It's the modern way, you said.
Then, on the street, you told the bishop
that what the city needed
was a proper cathedral
where important people could attend
the funerals of important people.
After they had died, you specified.
The horse looked more like a statue of a horse
than a horse per se,
and yet it was alive.
In fact, it smiled,
clearly disposed to being mounted,
happy for you to climb back on.
And once you've ridden off
your cheery wave
is all that's left between us.

newsworthy
Dave Clark

As the Indian space rocket
        PSLV-C37 launched 104 satellites
in a single flight
and Senators vowed to investigate
        Russian collusion and Valentine's Day chocolates
on sagging shelves
were reduced to half price
        and two bombs exploded
in north-west Pakistan and twenty-one organisers of
Eurovision resigned and the Pope
        pontificated and Venezuela banned the
CNN channel and New Zealand faced fires,

Dad died.

Only one of these
        was newsworthy

things left behind
Jordan Bryant

While cleaning out my grandmother's house
I sort through her treasures:
      her first teacup,
      her brother's WWII Navy uniform,
      her collection of cameos and
      cross stitch patterns

When I find her favorite mug,
the one with green florals at the rim
I think,

Oh no

She forgot to take this with her.

alma
Melody Rose Serra

They say the ebb and flow of time can heal all. But here I am still missing you. I hold onto the beautiful moments and also onto the moments where I learned you were my real-life hero. Alma: means soul in my native tongue. The most beautiful soul, my tia, my auntie, no longer with me on this earth. I remember the time you took me skiing for the first time, before you got sick. You taught me that fearless does not mean the absence of fear, but rather taking steps forward despite the fear. As you held my hand, overlooking an endless sea of ponderosa pines, you said, "together, every step." I know you were just trying to get me to try something new, but it felt like a promise, and trusting you'd keep it was easy. At every chemo appointment we went to together, I always brought you red vines and you'd hug me like it was the best gift ever. No matter the day, no matter the time, no matter how awful you felt, you approached the world with an openness and wonder. I watched as you asked the nurse how her daughter was doing, somehow remembering the details like what college her daughter was attending and what her name was. I sometimes wondered how you were real, how could someone be so beautiful? They say the ebb and flow of time can heal all. But here I am still missing you.

two candles
Burt Rashbaum

for Sharon

One out suddenly
        snuffed — gone — barely
a wisp of smoke
        like an echo
        of the flame
        all that remains

that burned so fiercely
        bright with the whole
        spectrum of color
and lasted through
        many seasons of darkness
but not nearly enough

    so now

now the room
        is half-lit — dimmed
as the other still
        burns
lighting the night
        til the sun returns.

runaway
Eben E. B. Bein

We were both [young/old/the age you'd expect] when
we ran away from home.
We imagined a home with [less/more] [chores/cookies/Commandments].
It was ['63/'97/'20].
We tossed [some cookies/a lighter/an alarm clock]
into the [bandana/car] for the trip.
We [took/left] our brothers too. We loved them un[equivocally/equally].
We left our mother [a/no] note saying exactly where we were going.
She suspected everything anyway.
We wondered what it meant to belong [to ourself/to somebody/.]
It took until sun[down/day/burn] to consider our error.
God, Mom, we were so [green/blue/red].
When we [lowered/tossed] our
[worries/bandana] out the window,
the [alarm clock/Commandments] broke.
Anger. Innocence overlaid.
What we ran from.
At times, we speak as though
we will [always/never] go back.

oh body!
Emily Moon

Where do you go
when I vanish into
the cave of my thoughts?
When I'm
lost in oblivion
planning, musing,
obsessing, who pumps
your heart? Who moves
your breath, makes
your blood flow,
your stomach gurgle?

How do we get
to where we need
to be?

keeper of the shelter tree
Chad Norman

All the clock's hour does, controlling us,
along with the best of the robins' singers.

New growth seems to be chosen perches
no matter how temporary the wind makes them.

Old inner boy, older on the outside now,
always wears white when heat has days.

Surrounded finally, not by common bills,
no, by a variety of seasonable beaks.

All seem to be as alive as he is,
only branches are chosen not untanned arms.

A theft took place due to ongoing downpours,
blossoms taken for crimson-cloud fragrance.

He claims he can see our planet's orbit
when wings share a single feather.

Perhaps it is a trick the sky plays out,
any weather always being on the line.

Swaying is practice by leaves any time of day,
how the wind teaches each one to join in.

He has breakthrough in his chosen cup,
to be keeper of the shelter tree.

No demands the kind money always wants,
each feathered visitor comes for free.

He continues to desire any connection,
offering a safety and mystery called trust.

To think years ago a brace was installed,
no one knew it was named, "Hawthorne."

domesticus tranquilis
John Dorroh

I like towns whose streets are named for trees —
Elm, Olive, Cypress, their canopies spreading
tender clutch above the rooftops
of homes that pulse with life: sleepy drivers
leaving protected carports before the sun infuses
its muted light through uncurtained windows.
Robust Colombian wafting through thumb-sized
holes in neglected corners that someone forgot to patch
again last summer. The silent stuffed cheeks of the gray mouse
who just left her evidence in a torn bag of snacks,
potato chip crumbs strewn throughout the dresser drawer.
Squirrels tight-rope skidding across sagging utility lines
like gravity doesn't matter. And teenagers waking up
like zombies in tattered, smelly nests from wee-hour escapades,
praying it's the weekend with a car of their own.

I like to drive down tree-lined streets and make-believe
that I am one of them, just for a day, looking up
into naked branches at a gray-white sky, lifting my foot off the gas,
waiting for the fog to lift, for the other foot to drop.
It always does.

I like the way that some of them are labeled to let you know
what it is, its genus and species, always in Italics
since everyone speaks Latin these days. *Acer rubrum,
Quercus rubra, Picea pungens.* It is paramount to be able
to classify things and put them in their places. Like leaves.
It gives us some sort of short-term power, a way to complicate
the uncomplicated.

I like how the man on Sycamore Street is always grilling.
Except early in the morning when he's probably at the market
selecting his meat of the day. The trees above his house

are always yellow in the summer and are the first to fall
in August. Maybe they can't breathe.

And when I go into the city it makes me sad to see trees
lined up against glass-and-chrome buildings, forced to grow
in chemical soil, where noise from the interstate never stops.
They miss the rooftops and dogs that bark down the street in the fog,
the sounds of the school bus opening its hungry mouth to swallow
children until 3 o'clock when once again it spits them out
at 254 Oak Avenue.

remembering the island
Sarah Burns

We think we will remember the way the church bell strikes every hour.

Or the way the fresh Portuguese bread smells fresh out of the oven. Just like the fisherman who sailed to the island and brought the recipe.

We think we will remember where the cobblestones are flattened and more worn, where it's easier to cross the street in front of the red brick bank building.

Or maybe we will cross in front of the old bookstore with the newly added second-floor reading room that's so quiet and peaceful.

Or maybe we will remember to cross just straight in front of the toggery shop, where you can buy those famous red pants.

You might make your way over to the garden of The Atheneum and sit for a while on the wooden benches. Smell the fresh-cut grass, watch the remnants of the blue hydrangea as its once-rich color loses its brightness.

Or watch the orange lilies as they fade and the last days of summer pass you by, reminding you that autumn is just around the corner.

And you will remember, as you walk back across the flattened cobblestones and you feel the first chill of that new season.

[the faerie's ring]
Sarah Alarcio

hushed whispers of the wind.
silky tendrils of the blooms.

hand outstretched.
reach.
seek.

a jewel held aloft,
suspended,
in the pitch expanse above.

yearning
and searching.
ever searching.

can you hear?
do you feel?
must you think?

a heart nonstop.
a want of pause.

do you know?
do you understand?

reflect.
ripple.
double-sided edge.

listen. listen. listen.

esteem i will wield.
from blackened anguish, bear this shield.

for who else can i love but you?

shadorma #1
P.Christine

Syllables
Without division
Are a mob,
Parts unknown,
Pretending they are something
They can never be.

looking for clues
Robert Pegel

Have a sneaky suspicion that
reincarnation is
real. People get more
time in different circumstances
maybe even different roles.
I told my deceased son that
next time — if he wants — he'll be the
father, I'll be the son. It's
fine as long as we
get another chance. We shouldn't
attach too much
to how things end
in this life. Take a deep breath.
More is on the way. The story may
have just begun
or we may be right in the
middle of it.

but I digress
Todd Matson

I want
to tell you,
but this is so
different from
anything I've ever
known, and I don't know
how you'll respond, what you'll
say, because there was always a comma,
no matter how hard I tried, always a "but," or
an "if only," or a "nevertheless," or a "nonetheless,"
or an "even so," or a "however," or a "but still," or an
"in spite of all that," or a "notwithstanding," or a "despite
that," or "for all that," or an "all the same," or a "just the same,"
or an "at the same time," or a "be that as it may," or an "although,"
or an "except for," or an "apart from," or an "other than," or an "aside
from," or "with the exception of," or a "short of," or a "barring that," or an
"excluding," or an "omitting," or a "leaving out," or a "save for," so don't you
see, there was nothing I could ever do, nothing I ever did, nothing I could ever be
that was ever good enough, you know, there was always a comma hanging over my
head, always a comma to punctuate my deficiency, always, always that tiny devastating
comma to say "almost, but not quite," there was always a comma, never a period. I love you.

amygdala
John Tessitore

The condition of love is the motion
of waves, the fall and rise, steady never still.
The ancients assumed its source in the heart,
the pulse, the rapid coursing and rush from
chest to limb. The brain, without a muscle
of its own, did not match their experience,
the ache, the flutter and twitch of desire.
I have tried to be quiet and mindful,
to sit on my pillow, stare at my wall,
but there is no end to the movement,
the pumping, the doubling of the rhythm.
Love plays itself to exhaustion, then plays
itself again. Perpetual beginning.
A love song is a melody repeating.

our place
Sandra Salinas Newton

Earth is quiet, slumbering under the relentless sun
Whose anger dissipates into the dusty, crimson soil.
What lives below has fed on fallen flesh and bloodless bone
And knows its life will, in its turn, do quite the same.
What else do we live for
                        Except to nourish the future?

So if we put an ear to the ground, or go barefoot,
We might know the sound and feel of teeming life
Beneath us:
                The scurry of colonies obeying their queen,
The writhing ecstasy of brainless worms
The slimy trail of blind slugs digging toward daylight.
What else can we do
                      Except applaud our discovery?

We congratulate ourselves for our cleverness,
Our striving to knowledge
                          Our gamut of emotions
But we forget
                Except perhaps alone, in the dark,
That our pulsing hearts and hectic brains will one day feed
The ants, the worms, the slugs, and all the life
On earth, in earth, under sky, in sky, underneath and overhead,
For we are simply fodder for the universe.

pineapple stain
Eric Burgoyne

The blood dropped in crimson
dots easily wiped away
though gone the pain remained

amber shaded, the textured pineapple
skin's rounded cuts always most difficult
each point of the diamond shapes

so easily broken while hand cutting
swearing and hoping the neighbors
didn't hear through open windows

crown leaves bold but simple
deadly large, jade hued shards
angled with emerald as complement

bold waves of cerulean meshed
with Persian blue carefully soldered
below azure and sapphire sky pieces

forming a cloud hinted heaven
twenty years hence my finger stings
of surgical slice and burn of molten lead

while gazing at the prickly glass fruit
in the transom above still hovering
between heaven and earth

the muse's knot
Karla Linn Merrifield

Hardware, as on a sloop,
prompts me to taut lines.
I cinch thoughts of you,
cleet my body so it yields
not an inch closer. Chrome
capstans? My polished spools
to wind words tightly
into reticence. At the loose
end of a long coiled sheet,
weathered, abraded raw
along one brief stretch,
I tie my first-figure-eight
knot and it tongue-ties me.
I take an inventory of hiding
places, hatches with shiny
hasps, the vee-berth with
no brass lamp to see by.
You won't hear me;
you can't read this.
With all its gleaming fittings,
all that metal, no line lax,
the sailboat tacks toward shore
in our glaring silence.

Zeus' garden
Amir Deen

He tended toward walking through the garden in old
Age. Strong yet strange in his growing lack of certainty
Servants no longer pleased him in recent days —
Days that seemed no different than those passed.
Hitherto he was a divine despot,
An antihero of a different path
Pleading with himself for a new development
In the story.
The man would sit next to his fountain
Wade his hand through the water
And try not to recognize the reflection
He saw. So he grabbed his bronze
Discus and dropped it like a dish.
Scanned the water until he
Found his face and said:
"I wish to forget the reflection of that man,
For I intend to be something much different."

six trips to Sirius
Adora Williams

The high priestess is facing boreas
I sat on that chair of black, white, and Rosegardens
Not every blue remains holy: the twin flames go red
Burst and break

The love of Hades and Persephone is misunderstood
Heliacal events are mere illusions from a past that
Still remains in our eyes that invoked the vision
Of the infinity to an end
And the colors multiply one another
Instead of creating the novelty

I love quatrains or measuring units to the shape of the sound
I always break them, though
On my sixth trip to Sirius, I found that Orion's belt was fading
And Artemis felt sorry for the death of Erato

The celestial sphere has corners and the remote corners of
An architect who liked to play with balls and set no pillars
To sustain the possibility of his creation creating another
Creation that would create that would —

Three levels of the rainbow body and I'm still here
Not knowing anything about what I am doing
But that's what coalesces the pieces of the puzzle

Satori, fanciful and nonchalant
Estivating in derailed circumstances

In the poetica of all time

centaurs in honey
Daniel A. Rabuzzi

Pliny The Elder reported in his <u>Natural History</u> (VII, iii) that he had seen a centaur preserved in honey, sent to Rome from Egypt.

What the eye sees confounds the eye even as the mind blinks

    and blinks

    and swallows. In a viscosity of sensation,
    our defenses submerged,
    slowly we engulf reason (too tart, an acerbic berry), sweetening the digestion of doubt.

Conviction thus preserved,
    we send forth — with industry — a thousand messengers to further instruct
    in the art of the impossible and the lure of the improbable.

Conjuring creatures into existence
    through strenuous application of will, later riding them
    to extinction in the wild, while displaying them in the canopic jars of our imagination.

the olive caper
Lisa MacKenzie

Before the cocktail party started
before her mom put on her heels and her "company" apron with the violets
before she heard doorbells and Herb Alpert on the stereo
before she heard grown-ups laughing and drinks clinking
before she smelled cigarette smoke mixed with perfume and aftershave
before she was firmly tucked into bed
before there were any guests at all
but after the hors d'oeuvres had been put out,
she tiptoed down to the living room
nightgowned and barefoot
and ate all the black olives.

favorite beverage
Logan Roberts

being simple, like simply light.
Too sweet, it's interpreted as sadness.

Or sour. For half an hour, I say the word *sour*
until it loses its flavor. I hold it in my hand, like a

stillborn puppy. Like the world, spinning on broken
toes into infinite darkness. Into limbo, sleep awkward

between death. I say this because
the truth is lodged, biting in the back

of my throat. I had a dream where I was a barista
but it had nothing to do with coffee

and everything to do with the high-quality
scent of you walking into a room. A room

full of furniture. Furniture we handpicked
together. Remember how it was delivered

in the pouring rain? That's how I remember it,
how I choose to drift in and out of us

being *us*. Like a real thing, a thing you show off
at reunions and Christmas parties.

Something that doesn't sink to the bottom
of a fancy glass, something that shines,

not too bright, perfectly encapsulating
everything we dared to talk about.

aromantic aromatic

R Hamilton

their's was a love affair
that sundered, the remains
of the fray reduced to
flotsam and jetsam
advancing and retreating
over and over and again
on the rocky shore in the
rough surf, yet still she
keeps looking for an unbroken
bottle semi-buried in the sand
with a washed-up wish for
reconciliation and apology
uncurling inside | the biting
smell of the salt spray gets
into her wounds, making them
worse, adding ache to ache: an
intractable ambergris of loss
ladled by the clumsy keening
of gulls into thin puddles
with wicks too short to burn
long enough for any warmth

noting nothing
Viktor Tanaskovski

No thing would be sacred if
scared of being scarred,

Think not you should knot each thing
With threads of foolish wit.

Though the right path could be tough,
Wittiness will find its witness.

Then the bitter taste will taste better than
Dinner lacking dessert in a desert diner.

Now that you know how,
Can it while you can;

Keep away from the keen
Narrow views, sly to the marrow.

Very few of them will vary,
Some will ever stay the same;

And the way they used to be used to use is, in the end,
Quite an easy way to quit and keep quiet.

If they don't back off of it,
Culture will become a vulture.

Older overt occult cults compulsively obsessed over order -
Feed not its need with a seed of their deed.

Could your synapses reveal the synopsis behind the cloud?
An aesthetic anesthetic cures this curse.

box
Terra Kestrel

This is the box. This is the only box. This is the box. There are other boxes. There are no other boxes. There is only this box. This is the only box.

This is the box in which you lean against the walls in fatigue and despair and hope and love and anger and hatred and violence and beauty. This is the box in which you hide in the corners listening to the loud crash of your tears against the floor. This is the box that you fill with the thing that is you. This is the box in which you do not fit, that presses against you, holding you, constricting you, crushing you.
This is the box in which you spend the nights crying.

This is the box that is you. This is the box that you are. This is the box that defines you. There are no other boxes. There is only this box. This is the box in which you fit.

This is the box. And the box is small. And the box is you. And the box is empty. And the box is filled with whiteness. Such a tiny amount of whiteness. Such a great expanse of whiteness. This is the box in which you put the tip of your pen. This is the box in which you make a small, black mark in the whiteness. This is the box. This is the box that is you. This is the only box. There are other boxes.

There are no other boxes.

I am the spell
Maura Alia Badji

I am the Spell, the deep,
the dark
under-curve of the Moon. The path
taken late
or too soon. Understand,
I am all the songs, you know
by heart. I am
the core of the soul, left to wither,
yet bloomed. I am
my arcane name deep inscribed
in rhyme, long
out of synch, out of time
still in tune.
I am the Spell, underlined
just in time,
out of sight, out of mind
suddenly materialized
in thin air. Blood close,
as the breakbeats of your heart,
as the lines of your palms,
I linger, as the echo of your song.
Insistently glowing,
I push through the cheap
illusion of gloom.

an ode to my first internet friend
Kelli Lage

for Justyna

Stored draft of us,
parading unripened hillsides,
baring our teeth to unfractured sun.

We lift chins
when our animals hook sunlight.
We bathe our pores in art.
We cheer for bodies and celebrate the living.

You, in film reels.
Me, flipping through polaroids.

I'll meet you *jutro*.
We can take in each other's faces
and act out the rest of our lives.

Jutro — tomorrow (Polish)

you wish a heartbeat would suffice
Samikchhya Bhusal

you clean the kitchen drawers & search for a country
tidy up the apartment & look for pieces of your old self
fold your laundry & the same smell of cheap detergent
you can no longer trace your mother's perfume

even in your dreams, someone wants your permanent address
& you sleep talk affirmations until you can dream again
puzzle them, confuse them, distract them
tell them your body is your home

you fill out paperwork *How long*
have you been in the US? What was the
purpose of your visit? How
long have you been together? Where
did you meet? our bodies are dangerous &

everything else is safe
the cops/the wars/the prisons/the floods
this list is long enough to reach

your mother across the continent but the
immigration officer won't
let go
love is not a polite houseguest

no signs of arrival or departure
no falling of leaves, rain, snow
yesterday, he was playing with your hair
writing you love poems, mailing you gifts
holding your hands
gently, he left.

past life lighthouse
Megan Gahart

I've always believed that I was a lighthouse keeper
in a past life,
not because I could look back through the years
as if flipping the pages of a book,
but because I've never passed a lighthouse
and not felt compelled to go in,
didn't matter if it was the new, metallic red
more jarring than captivating
or the intricate, crumbling brick
eroded by at least a century,
a place I'd known my whole life
that felt like home or one across the country,
alluring in its foreignness.
I never stopped myself from committing
to each metal clanking footstep
drawn to the colossal bulb
glass shimmering even when unlit
as if I would find a piece of myself there,
even knowing that the descent would take twice as long
with trembling legs and panicked, heaving breaths,
the see-through spiral stairs a constant reminder
of the distance to the ground.
I've stared at each photograph in every attached museum
searching for a sign of myself like in a family album,
listened to every tour guide tell the stories
like it's my biography,
but maybe I've always just been drawn to that light
circling like loving arms outstretched,
the thought of someone there all night to offer guidance
whether a ship trying to find its way
or a lone soul unable to sleep in the wake of longing,
looking out the window to find that dependable beam.
Maybe I just want someone to climb to the top

thinking of me with each step,
to fight off sleep hour after hour
to ensure the flame never dies,
to sit there all night and keep the light on for me.

my children will be dead before their 50th birthday
Sarah Groustra

You never know what you're going to see until you've seen it
"and isn't that the way?"
There will be, someday,
the chocolate ice cream and cotton candy of perpetual youth
but for now it's just another night, seeking solace
in the emptiness
in the wonders that are not for me
"You must be this tall to ride"
I don't want to feel guilty for craving fullness
but I was born too late
"and isn't that the way?"

mending
Katie E. Peckham

she's working
to stitch together

the fine figure he cut
with the marks his hand left behind —

to straighten the hem
because the cloth falls on the bias —

to pin the butterflies
to the inflammation —

like Wendy sewing on
Peter Pan's shadow

so that in the end
it will fit true to size

to a whale bobbing rhythmically in the surf
Jacob Riyeff

>   *fisc flodu ahof on fergenberig;*
>   *warþ gasric grorn, þær he on greut giswom.*

>   *the fish piled up waters on faces of rock;*
>   *the fearsome king grew sad, swam on the shingle.*

>   — *Franks Casket*

Incessant marine furling and unfurling,
two otters glistening oiled barges,
spiked fields of clawberry succulents,
ocean breeze, ropey roots,
moor in miniature of yellow flowers.
And you're away down in the cove,
deep-cut wales furrowing your belly,
white spattered tail sways and the bloat
of your corpse says no life is left
in you. Vultures won't yet alight
on your hide, but they ride the cliff currents
in the midday sun above and around
your watery limbs. And the waves rotate your body,
your massive head a cold pivot:
the purple blossoms trembling hundreds
of feet above your freakish and lovely bulk.

madam ocean
Krista Bergren-Walsh

Adorned with pearls
and multicolored
sea glass woven into
necklaces, she basks in
warm sunlight
filtering through the
translucent surface down
cerulean sapphire waters.

Throughout murky depths
the songs from whales echo,
filling the ocean with their
melodies and lamentations.

She still knows where
to find healthy colorful
reefs, dances with
shimmering schools
of fish, explores sunken,
rust covered ships.

She is the ocean,
a body filled with
life and death, decorated
in bioluminescence.

harvest moon haibun
Nicole Callräm

there is a color to every day like scales on a giant fish we inhabit; so much depends on the light of a sun or moon touching curve and surface —green blushes, sighs, melts to butter. the bluebird grows new feathers each autumn, shocking sapphire plumes framed by hues of corn and straw. you are this act of rebellion. reincarnation as a foil to life's slow destruction. when we met I noticed a spike of wheat stuck — a sun ray in the sleeve of that black sweater. you blushed. said there was a field behind the school you loved to lose yourself in, grass so tall it brushed your lips. I wish I could gather September, golden heads of wheat, blue feathers, and how you looked that day — make a wine so deep it would taste of earth herself.

    sweet fruit harvest's heart. sky soft year slowing to end. I thirst for it all.

stars
Kerry Darbishire

I can speak up for my habitat
when all is cascading around me

I can stop mowing the lawn
when concrete stands in for fields

I can keep feeding the birds
when trains bulldoze hedges

I can catch rain from gutters
hold the colour green

the summer long and when all
is parched I can recall the scent

of petrichor, bluebells, falling leaves
remember how I took them for granted

I can bring you a song thrush singing
through early morning rain

leaves unfurling pink in the oak
I can write a poem to save someone

and I will show you a summer river
brimmed with stars

biographies

Sarah Wallis is based in Scotland, UK, and publishes cross-genre. Some of her published works include the chapbooks Medusa Retold, Precious Mettle, and How to Love the Hat Thrower. Highlights include the staging of her works in The Rain King and Laridae and having works in The Yorkshire Poetry Anthology. She is thrilled to have works in various sea-themed literary journals this year as the ocean is her muse and delight. You can find her @wordweave on Twitter.

Pamela Nocerino is a ghostwriter, actor, and teacher who once helped build a giant troll in the Rocky Mountains. She enjoyed a brief career on stage in Denver until she needed health insurance and became a dedicated middle school teacher. Her poetry credits include Gyroscope Review, Plum Tree Tavern, Splintered Disorder Press, Third Estate Art's Quaranzine, Writing in a Woman's Voice, Capsule Stories, and Minnow Literary Magazine. Pamela's fiction credits include two short plays and a short story in Jerry Jazz Musician.

William G. Gillespie lives and writes in Brooklyn, NY. His poetry has appeared in *Olney Magazine*, *Red Eft Review,* and *The Drunken Canal*.

Lulu Liu is a writer and physicist, who lives between Arlington, Massachusetts, and Parsonsfield, Maine. Her writing has appeared in the Technology Review and Sacramento Bee, among others, and recently her poetry in Apple Valley Review, and Thimble. She's grateful to be nominated for Best of the Net 2023.

Liz Pino Sparks is a writer, legal scholar, educator, and mami to five. She lives with her partner, also a writer and educator, children, and pets in the Southwest.

Michigan-born **Moira Walsh** makes her home in southern Germany and translates for a living. You can find her poems in Bennington Review, Denver Quarterly, Poetry Northwest, Sip Cup, Storm Cellar, and elsewhere.

Carella Keil is a poet and digital artist who splits her time between the ethereal world of dreams, and Toronto, Canada, depending on the weather. Her work involves themes of mental health, nature and sexuality, often in a surrealist tone. Carella is the recipient of the Stanley Fefferman Prize in Creative Writing (2006) and 2nd place winner in the Open Minds Quarterly BrainStorm Poetry Contest (2017). Recently, she has been published in Margins Magazine, Wrongdoing Magazine, Shuf Poetry, Myth & Lore and Solstice Literary Magazine. Forthcoming publications include Paddler Press, Fragmented Voices, Querencia Press, Stripes

Literary Magazine, Door is a Jar, Deep Overstock, Writeresque, Free Verse Revolution and Burningword.

Candice Kelsey teaches writing in the South. Her poetry appears in Poets Reading the News and Poet Lore among other journals, and her first collection, Still I am Pushing, explores mother-daughter relationships as well as toxic body messages. She won the Two Sisters Writing Contest for her micro story, was chosen as a finalist in Cutthroat's Joy Harjo Poetry Prize, and was recently nominated for both a Best of the Net and two Pushcarts.

Karina Fantillo is a storyteller and dancer. She learned about her Philippine roots and American culture through folk dancing as a teenager in San Francisco, where she immigrated with her family as a child. She left her senior year of college to raise her niece and become her legal guardian. Twenty years later, Karina finished her BA in English at the University of San Francisco, where she also earned an MFA in Writing.

Melanie Taing (she/her) is the daughter of Cambodian genocide survivors, the event from which most of her stories are inspired. Some of these include two plays: *Lost in Translation* and *Apsongha,* and short fiction including: *The Art of Folding Pink* and *When the Sun Dies*. A UCLA alum and recent grad of the SDSU MFA program, her current manuscript revolves around intergenerational trauma within the Cambodian diaspora. She runs a small craft business and is obsessed with music, karaoke, houseplants, astronomy, mental health advocacy, tea and her Schnauzer-Terrier pup, Oliver, aka Olliepop.

Shari Lawrence Pfleeger's poems reflect both natural and constructed worlds, often describing interactions with family and friends. Her regular essays on poetry appear in Blue House Journal, and her poems have been published in District Lines, Thimble Literary, Blue House Journal, Green Light, Paper Dragon, Boats Against the Current, and in four anthologies of Yorkshire poetry. Her prize-winning collection of Yorkshire sonnets was launched in Britain 2021 at the Fourth Ripon Poetry Festival. Shari is on the board of Alice James Books, a poetry press committed to producing, promoting, and distributing poetry that engages the public on important social issues. She lives, writes, and rides her bicycle in Washington, DC.

Rebecca Siegel lives and writes in Vermont. Her poems have appeared in *Moist Poetry Journal, Bloodroot Literary Magazine, Pinhole Poetry, Boats Against the Current, Visual Verse, Dust Poetry Magazine, Analog Magazine, Zócalo Public Square,* and elsewhere.

Lisa Bickmore is the author of three books of poems. The second, *flicker* (2016), won the 2014 Antivenom Prize from Elixir Press. She won the 2015 Ballymaloe International Poetry Prize for the poem "Eidolon," which appears in her third collection, *Ephemerist* (2017, Red Mountain Press). She is the founder and publisher of the new independent nonprofit Lightscatter Press. In July 2022, she was named the Poet Laureate for the state of Utah.

Emily Updegraff lives near Chicago with her family and their dog, Coco. She has published in *Third Wednesday, The Orchards Poetry Journal,* and *River and South Poetry Review*. She is a regular book review contributor at *Great Lakes Review.*

Laura Bonazzoli's poetry has appeared in dozens of literary magazines, including *Connecticut River Review*, *Northern New England Review*, and *SLANT*, as well as in four anthologies and on "Poems from Here" on Maine Public Radio. She has also published personal essays and fiction. Her short-story cycle, *Consecration Pond*, was published by indie press Toad Hall Editions in August of 2022.

Kelli Weldon was born and raised in Louisiana and now resides in Texas. She studied journalism and literature at Northwestern State University in Natchitoches, Louisiana, and served on the editorial board of its literary magazine, Argus. Find her poetry in publications including Eclectica Magazine and In Parentheses.

Sonja Crone *1982 in Speyer am Rhein (Germany) lives in Oberwil near Basel (Switzerland). She is a poet and artist and also works as an editor. Her texts as well as paintings have so far been published in various anthologies, e.g. Versnetze_14 und 15 (Verlag Ralf Liebe, 2021) on online platforms and in literary and art magazines, including Der Dreischneuß, Haller, Das Goetheanum, Der Maulkorb, Kalmenzone, Denkbilder, erostepost and Stadtgelichter.

Ivan de Monbrison is a poet and artist living in Paris born in 1969, with Jewish Russian, Tcherkess and Arabic roots, and affected by various types of mental disorders.

Clara McShane is a writer from Dublin with a BA in Psychology. She has been writing for most of her life, and finds a sense of peace and balance from engaging with poetry and prose. Her work has appeared in various publications such as The Ogham Stone, The Caterpillar Magazine, and Chasing Shadows, a Creative Ireland Poetry Anthology edited by Noel Monahan.

Peter Chiu lives in the San Gabriel Valley with his wife.

Lisa Molina is an educator/writer in Austin, Texas. She is a "2022 Best of the Net" nominee for her poem "Who You See," published in *Fahmidan Journal,* and her digital chapbook "Don't Fall in Love With Sisyphus," published by Fahmidan Publishing, launched in February 2022. Her words can be found in numerous journals, including *boats against the current magazine, The Ekphrastic Review, Beyond Words Magazine, Sky Island Journal,* and *Neologism Poetry Journal.*

Kerry Darbishire has always lived in the English Lake District where most of her poetry is rooted. Her poems appear in many anthologies and magazines worldwide. She has two pamphlets published by Dempsey & Windle and a collaboration with Kelly Davis published by Grey Hen Press. Her first full collection with Indigo Dreams Publishing and her third collection Jardinière was published by Hedgehog Press in June 2022.

M.R. Mandell is a writer and actress living in Los Angeles. A transplant from Katy, Texas, she now lives by the beach with her muse, a Golden Retriever named Chester Blue (always at her feet), and her longtime partner. She studies poetry at the Lighthouse Writers Workshop in Denver, and The Writing Salon, San Francisco. You can find her work in anthologies by Wingless Dreamer Publishers, Pile Press's summer issue, The Dried Review's premiere edition, and Vine Leaves Press '50 Give or Take' (2023).

Jose Hernandez Diaz is a 2017 NEA Poetry Fellow. He is the author of The Fire Eater (Texas Review Press, 2020). His work appears in The American Poetry Review, Boulevard, Crazyhorse, Georgia Review, Huizache, Iowa Review, The Missouri Review, Poetry, The Southern Review, Witness Magazine, The Yale Review, and in The Best American Nonrequired Reading Anthology 2011. He teaches creative writing online and edits for Frontier Poetry.

Natalie Bühler is an emerging writer living on Gadigal Land in Sydney, Australia, originally from Switzerland. She works at the Sydney-based poetry organization Red Room Poetry and incorporates her native Swiss German, which does not have a standardized written form, into her English writing. Her work has appeared in *Tint Journal*.

Jeannie Marschall is a teacher from the green center of Germany who also writes stories, time permitting. She enjoys long walks with her dog and cat, foraging, and tending her semi-sentient vegetable garden while inventing tall tales with her partner, or huddling around the fire in their witches' hut for the same purpose. Jeannie mostly writes SciFi and all kinds of colorful Fantasy stories as well as the odd poem. She has a few short pieces lined up for publication this year, for example with Black Spot Books, The Banshee Journal, and QueerWelten magazine. Longer works are in the pipeline.

Gina Gidaro (she/her) is a creative writing graduate who loves reading, playing video games, watching Asian dramas, and being with family. Several of her stories, poems, and photographs have appeared in magazines and online zines. If she's not obsessing over other people's stories, she's probably writing her own... or eating an excessive amount of fudge brownies. Her ultimate dream is to become a successful novelist.

Debbie Robson loves to write fiction set in the first sixty years of the last century. She has had stories published in Vestal Review, Many Nice Donkeys, Serious Flash and others and poetry in Boats Against the Current, Ethelzine, Emerge Journal and more. She tweets @lakelady2282.

Kathryn Sadakierski is a 23-year-old writer whose work has been published in anthologies, magazines, and literary journals around the world, including Agape Review, Critical Read, Halfway Down the Stairs, Literature Today, NewPages Blog, Northern New England Review, seashores: an international journal to share the spirit of haiku, Snapdragon: A Journal of Art and Healing, Yellow Arrow Journal, and elsewhere. Her micro-chapbook "Travels through New York" was published by Origami Poems Project (2020). Kathryn collects vinyl records, vintage books, and memories, which inspire her art. She graduated summa cum laude with a B.A. and M.S. from Bay Path University in Longmeadow, Massachusetts.

Sean Patrick is a scientist and sonnet aficionado. Their poetry has appeared in *Grand Little Things, UniVerses, Blue Unicorn,* and *Lavender Lime Literary*.

Kara Dunford (she/her) is a writer living in Washington, DC. She serves as Poetry Editor for Overtly Lit. Find her on Twitter @kara_dunford.

C. Heyne (any/all) is a genderqueer poet from Sunrise, Florida, and resides in Hoboken, NJ. C is the recipient of the William Morgan Poetry Award and has poems featured or forthcoming in Muse/A, DreamPOP, The Oakland Review, Identity Theory, The Bullshit Anthology, and Kiss Your Darlings, amongst others. Their chapbook "my room (and other wombs)" is forthcoming (Bullshit Lit, 2023).

Jessica Berry grew up beside the seaside in Bangor, Northern Ireland. She currently works as an English teacher in Belfast. In 2021, Jessica was placed in Bangor's annual poetry contest hosted by the Aspects Literary Festival and recently she placed second at the Fingal Poetry Festival slam. Her work has also been included in publications such as Drawn to the Light, A New Ulster, and Rust & Moth.

Ryan Diaz is a poet and writer from Queens, NY. He holds a BA in History from St. Johns University and is currently completing a MA in Biblical Studies. His work has been featured in publications like *Ekstasis, Premier Christianity, Dappled Things*, and Common Good Mag. He is the author of two poetry books, *For Those Wandering Along the Way,* and *Skipping Stones*. Ryan's writing attempts to find the divine in the ordinary, the thin place where fantasy and reality meet. He currently lives in Queens, NY with his wife Janiece.

Carver Bain is a writer, baker, and gardener. He grew up in Washington State and received a degree from Johns Hopkins University in the Writing Seminars. He lives in California with his fiancée, as well as his two cats, Sylvia and Fran.

Kimberly Reiss is a licensed psychotherapist and writer. She is the creator of the Motherhood Selfhood workshop series and is now creating the corresponding workbook of the same name. Kimberly is a co-author of an award-winning play entitled, *Man In The Flying Lawnchair,* which was included in Best Plays of 2000. It appeared in The Edinburgh Fringe Festival (where it won the prestigious Fringe First Award), and was re-recorded as a radio play for the BBC. Kimberly created and produced *The Go Girl! Film Festival,* focusing on issues facing teenage girls. Kimberly is currently writing a memoir, "Fall to Grace." She divides her time between Austin and Los Angeles.

Louis Faber is a poet, photographer, and blogger. His work has appeared in The Whisky Blot, The Poet (U.K.), Alchemy Spoon, New Feathers Anthology, Dreich (Scotland), Tomorrow and Tomorrow, Erothanatos (Greece), Defenestration, Atlanta Review, Glimpse, Rattle, Cold Mountain Review, Eureka Literary Magazine, Borderlands: the Texas Poetry Review, Midnight Mind, Pearl, Midstream, European Judaism, The South Carolina Review and Worcester Review, among many others, and has been nominated for a Pushcart Prize.

Erica Abbott (she/her) is a Philadelphia-based poet and writer whose work has previously appeared or is forthcoming in Button Poetry, Midway Journal, Kissing Dynamite, Serotonin, The Broadkill Review, and other journals. She is the author of *Self-Portrait as a Sinking Ship*, is a Best of the Net nominee, and volunteers for Button Poetry, Write or Die Tribe, and Variant Literature. Follow her on Instagram @poetry_erica and on Twitter @erica_abbott.

Annie Marhefka is a writer in Baltimore, Maryland. Her creative nonfiction and poetry have been published by Hobart, Literary Mama, Pithead Chapel, Anti-Heroin Chic, and others. Annie is the Executive Director at Yellow Arrow Publishing, a Baltimore-based nonprofit supporting and empowering women writers, and is working on a memoir about mother/daughter relationships. You can find Annie's writing on Instagram @anniemarhefka and Twitter @charmcityannie.

Emma Lara Jones lives in Felixstowe, England. She has had many jobs including piano tutor, lawyer, and English teacher. She now focuses on her writing full-time and is about to begin a Creative Writing Master's degree.

Doryn Herbst, a former scientist in the water industry, Wales, now lives in Germany and is a deputy local councillor. Her writing considers the natural world but also themes that address social issues. Doryn has poetry in Fahmidan Journal, CERASUS Magazine, Fenland Poetry Journal, celestite poetry, and more. She is a reviewer at Consilience science poetry journal.

Devon Bohm received her BA from Smith College and earned her MFA with a dual concentration in Poetry and Fiction from Fairfield University. After serving as *Mason Road's* Editor-in-Chief, she worked as an adjunct professor of English. She was awarded the Hatfield Prize for Best Short Story, two honorable mentions in L. Ron Hubbard Writers of the Future Contest, and was longlisted for *Wigleaf*'s Top Very Short Fictions. Her work has also been featured in publications such as *Labrys, The Graveyard Zine, Horse Egg Literary, Necessary Fiction, Eunoia Review, Spry, Sixfold, Hole in the Head Review, orangepeel, Helix Magazine*, and Sunday Mornings at the River's *365 Days of Covid* anthology. Her first book of poetry, *Careful Cartography*, was published in 2021 by Cornerstone Press.

Beth Mulcahy is a Pushcart Prize-nominated poet whose work has appeared in various journals and her chapbook, *Firmer Ground*, is forthcoming with Anxiety Press. Beth lives in Ohio with her husband and two children and works for a company that provides technology to people without natural speech.

Alexis Renata is an emerging writer from the Pacific Northwest, now living in San Diego. She primarily writes speculative poetry and fiction. Her work is forthcoming in *Strange Horizons* and *Kaleidotrope*.

Bill Richardson is Emeritus Professor in Spanish at the University of Galway, Ireland. He has published books and articles on Spanish and Latin American literature and culture. Poems of his have been published in Irish newspapers, as well as in Atrium, The Galway Review, Pendemic, Vox Galvia, The Seventh Quarry, Amethyst Review, The Stony Thursday Book, Orbis, The Orchards, Book XI-A Journal of Literary Philosophy, and the Fish Anthology 2020.

Dave Clark is a writer-poet with CFS, living in Mparntwe (Alice Springs). He works as a counselor, giving voice to quieter stories. He won the 2022 NT Literary Award for Poetry and has works published in *Mascara, Imprint, Pure Slush, SwimMeet Lit, Selcouth Station, Melbourne Culture Corner*, and *Right Now*.

Jordan Bryant is a neurodivergent poet living in Indianapolis with her husband Josh and their dogs; Norman and Edgar.

Melody Rose Serra's passion is teaching and empowering others by sharing what she has learned. She helped launch an arts and crafts program at a children's hospital and also taught at San Quentin State Prison. Melody hopes to inspire youth to explore and expand their creativity through web development, writing, and art.

Burt Rashbaum's publications are *Of the Carousel* (The Poet's Press, 2019), and *Blue Pedals* (Editura Pim, 2015, Bucharest). His poems have appeared in *XY Files* (Sherman Asher Publishing, 1997), *The Cento* (Red Hen Press, 2011), *Art in the Time of Covid-19* (San Fedele Press, 2020), *A 21st Century Plague: Poetry from a Pandemic* (University Professors Press, 2021), *American Writers Review: Turmoil and Recovery* (San Fedele Press, 2021), and The Antonym. His fiction has appeared in Meet Cute Press, Caesura, Typeslash Review, Collateral, and *American Writers Review: The End or the Beginning* (San Fedele Press, 2022).

Eben E. B. Bein (he/they) is a high-school-biology-teacher-turned-climate-justice-educator at the nonprofit Our Climate. He is a 2022 Fellow for the "Writing By Writers Workshop," winner of the 2022 *Writers Rising Up "Winter Variations"* poetry contest, and has published poems in *Passenger's Journal, Thimble Lit, Wild Roof Journal*, and *Meat For Tea*. They are currently completing their first collection *"From the top of the sky"* which explores the weave of parent-child love and conflict. He lives on Pawtucket land (Cambridge, MA) with some ivy plants that are not dead because his husband remembers to water them. FB/T/IG @beinology.

Emily Moon (she/her) is a transgender poet from Portland, Oregon. She is Editor at First Matter Press. Her book, *It's Just You and Me, Miss Moon*, was published by First Matter Press prior to her taking on an editorial role. Her work includes appearances in or forthcoming from

Pile Press, Labyrinth Anthologies, Solstice Literary Magazine, En*gendered Literary Magazine, Ethel Zine, Variant Literature, Full House Literary, Celestite Poetry Journal, Wild Roof Journal, and elsewhere.

Chad Norman lives and writes in Truro, Nova Scotia. In 1992 he was awarded the Gwendolyn MacEwen Memorial Award For Poetry, the judges were Margaret Atwood, Barry Callaghan, and Al Purdy. His poems appear in journals, magazines, and anthologies around the world. A new book, *A Matter Of Inclusion* is out now.

John Dorroh has never fallen into an active volcano or caught a hummingbird. However, he managed to bake bread with Austrian monks and drink a healthy portion of their beer. Two of his poems were nominated for Best of the Net. Others appeared in journals such as Feral, River Heron, and Selcouth Station. His first chapbook comes out in 2022.

A native New Englander, writer, and activist, **Sarah Burns** lives and writes in Los Angeles, California. She has been writing poetry since the age of sixteen and is currently working on a memoir.

Sarah Alarcio is a Filipino-American musician, composer, vocalist, and writer currently residing in Arizona. She graduated from Northern Arizona University with a BA in Business Administration, Information Systems and a minor in Japanese. She mainly draws inspiration from music. In her free time, she can be found playing Final Fantasy XIV and espousing its virtues to her friends and family.

P.Christine is a handi-capable, lesbian poet. Born in California, she currently resides in the suburbs of Chicago. Her poetry evokes emotions about loss, philosophy, and social justice. She has been published in rez Magazine and The Fib Review. She is the recipient of two Sparta Open Mic awards.

Todd Matson is a Licensed Marriage and Family Therapist in North Carolina, United States. His poetry has been published in The Journal of Pastoral Care and Counseling; Soul-Lit: A Journal of Spiritual Poetry, and his short stories have been published in Ariel Chart International Literary Journal; Faith, Hope and Fiction; and Children, Churches and Daddies.

John Tessitore has been a newspaper reporter, a magazine writer, and a biographer. He has taught British and American history and literature at colleges around Boston and has directed national policy studies on education, civil justice, and cultural policy. Most recently, he has published poems in the *American Journal of Poetry*, *Canary*, *The Wallace Stevens Journal*, *The Ekphrastic Review*, *Wild Roof*, *Magpie Lit*, *The Closed Eye Open*, *Gastropoda* the *Sunday Mornings at the River* anthology and forthcoming in *Boats Against the Current* and the *Wee Sparrow* anthology.

Sandra Salinas Newton is a Filipina-American professor emeritus of English currently living in Austin, Texas. Her published work includes texts, essays, fiction, and currently poetry, in over forty online and print journals. She was recently one of four finalists in the 2022 Writers' League of Texas Manuscript Contest (Historical Fiction category). Twitter: @DocSSN.

Eric Burgoyne writes poetry from his home on the North Shore of Oahu, Hawaii. He has an MA in Creative Writing from Teesside University in Middlesbrough, England, and MBA from Reading University in Berkshire, England. His poems appear in Lothlorien Poetry Journal, The Dawntreader, and Paddler Press, among others.

Karla Linn Merrifield has had 1000+ poems appear in dozens of journals and anthologies. She has 15 books to her credit. Following her 2018 *Psyche's Scroll* (Poetry Box Select) is the full-length book *Athabaskan Fractal: Poems of the Far North* from Cirque Press. Her newest poetry collection, *My Body the Guitar*, nominated for the National Book Award, was inspired by famous guitarists and their guitars and published in December 2021 by Before Your Quiet Eyes Publications Holograph Series (Rochester, NY). She is a frequent contributor to *The Songs of Eretz Poetry Review*.

Amir Deen lives in San Diego and has a Bachelor's degree in Literature & Writing. He aspires to one day own a Chow Chow – whom he will go on beach walks, hikes, and whimsical adventures with.

Adora Williams has degrees in Journalism and Languages and has written poetry for 14 years. She lives in a historic region of Brazil. Her poetry anthology, Mulher Poesia, in Portuguese is being published in Brazil and Portugal in December 2022.

Daniel A. Rabuzzi (he / his) has had two novels, five short stories, twenty poems, and nearly 50 essays / articles published. He lived eight years in Norway, Germany, and France. He has degrees in the study of folklore & mythology and European history. He lives in New York City with his artistic partner & spouse, the woodcarver Deborah A. Mills, and the requisite cat. Tweets @TheChoirBoats.

Retired after 30 years as a human resources professional, **Lisa MacKenzie** is enjoying the free time in which to write poetry. Her work has appeared online at Visual Verse and Literary North. She lives in Maryland with her husband and cats.

Logan Roberts is an artist and writer in Florida. Tweets @hello_im_logan.

R Hamilton (they/them) began writing poetry in high school and was published in the 1970 literary magazine. Then: career, life, etc. Their next "published" piece was included in City Lights Theater's 2020 Halloween podcast, an unintentionally even number of years and decades. Pretty much sticking with writing for the time being, Hamilton's gap years provide much good material, especially when examined with a jaundiced eye.

Viktor Tanaskovski is a musician and a music teacher from Skopje, North Macedonia. He graduated with jazz guitar from "Goce Delcev" University in Stip in 2016, and at the moment he is studying for a Master's degree in Applied music research at the Faculty of Music in Belgrade, Serbia. Currently, he is working on his first book of poetry, which is about to be released by the end of 2022.

Terra Kestrel is an anthropologist and geographer. She writes speculative fiction and poetry often focusing on themes of equality, intergenerational trauma, love, hope, and healing. She lives in rural Oregon with her wife, children, and an embarrassingly large collection of fountain pens. Twitter: @terrakestrel.

Maura Alia Badji is a poet, writer, songwriter, editor, ESL teacher, and social services worker. Her writing has appeared in *Rogue Agent, The Skinny Poetry Review, Aeolian Harp, The Delaware Review, Pirene's Fountain, The Buffalo News, The Phoenix Soul, The Good Men Project, This City Is a Poem, Barely South Review*, and other publications. She has work forthcoming in *The Citron Review and Identity Theory*. She studied poetry at San Francisco State and earned her MFA at the University of WA, Seattle, where she was an Editorial Assistant at *The Seattle Review*. She is a Poetry Editor for *The Deaf Poets Society* and lives in Virginia Beach with her musician son, Ibrahim.

Kelli Lage is earning her degree in Secondary English Education and works as a substitute teacher. She is a poetry reader for Bracken Magazine. Lage's work has appeared in The Lumiere Review, Welter Journal, Watershed Review, and elsewhere. Instagram and Twitter: @KelliLage.

Samikchhya Bhusal writes to create places of home and hope. She grew up in Kathmandu and currently lives in Los Angeles. She works at a nonprofit to advance equitable mobility.

Megan Gahart is a Wisconsin native, currently studying English and Gender and Women's Studies at the University of Wisconsin-Madison. This is her first publication. @megangahart on Instagram and Twitter.

Sarah Groustra (she/her) is a senior at Kenyon College in Gambier, OH, where she studies English and drama. Her writing has previously appeared in Funicular Magazine, Lilith Magazine, and the Jewish Women's Archive. Her plays have been workshopped or produced by Playdate Theatre, the Parsnip Ship, Grub Street, and Playwright's Workshop at Kenyon (PWAK). Sarah is originally from Brookline, Massachusetts, and her favorite thing in the world is breakfast all day. You can find her on Twitter at @ladypoachedegg.

Katie E. Peckham writes and wonders in Los Angeles, in between building pillow forts with her kids and failing to keep up with the cilantro turning to slime in her fridge. She is a neurodivergent who has a deep and abiding love for underdogs. She has been published in *Running With Water* and *Quillkeepers' Autumn Anthology*.

Jacob Riyeff is a teacher, translator, and poet. His work focuses on the western contemplative tradition and the natural world. Jacob lives in Milwaukee's East Village with his wife and three growing children.

Krista Bergren-Walsh graduated from Creighton University in 2016 with a double major in both Creative Writing and Theatre Performance. Due to severe health issues and misdiagnoses for five years, Krista was unable to pursue either passion until recently. Since 2021, she has had poetry and flash fiction published by Wishbone Words, boats against the current, The Dalloway Press, voidspace zine, Moon Cola, and Storytellers Refrain. Krista has upcoming works in Bullshit Lit and The Bitchin' K, and won 6th place in the Writer's Digest 90th Annual Competition in Script/Screen Play Writing.

Nicole Callräm is a nomadic bureaucrat whose work has appeared or is forthcoming in journals such as Five South, The Night Heron Barks, Allium, and Kissing Dynamite. She is a poetry editor at ASPZ: A Shanghai Poetry Zine. She currently calls Shanghai home.

Kerry Darbishire has always lived in the English Lake District where most of her poetry is rooted. Her poems appear in many anthologies and magazines worldwide. She has two pamphlets published by Dempsey & Windle and a collaboration with Kelly Davis published by Grey Hen Press. Her first full collection is with Indigo Dreams Publishing and her third collection Jardinière was published by Hedgehog Press in June 2022.

McKenna Themm lives in San Diego and has an MFA in Creative Writing. Her poetry chapbook *Ever Yours, Vincent* — about the life and art of Vincent van Gogh — was published by *dancing girl press*. Her poems have been published in several journals, including *The Poet*, *Ekphrastic Review*, *Bryant Literary Review*, *pacificREVIEW*, and *The Headlight Review*, among others. She was nominated for the AWP Intro Journals 2022 Award and is a two-time Sarah Brenda Marsh-Rebelo scholarship recipient. She is the founder and editor-in-chief of the poetry magazine *boats against the current*.

Made in United States
Orlando, FL
27 November 2022